RAISING A WILD CHILD

GW00674274

RAISING A WILD CHILD

An Inside Perspective of a Neurodivergent
Mind and How to Parent Those Who
Cannot Be Parented

Suzan Issa

Copyright © 2023 by Suzan Issa

All rights reserved. No part of this book may be reproduced or used in any manner without written permission of the copyright owner except for the use of quotations in a book review. For more information, contact: suzan@suzanissa.com

First paperback edition 2023

Book design by Zahra Issa

ISBNs:
Paperback: 978-1-80541-266-3
eBook: 978-1-80541-267-0

https://raisingawildchild.co.uk

Introduction

There are a few things I'd like you to know about this book.

Firstly, it will not have chapters because it is mainly a series of thoughts. Some of these won't be long enough for my autistic brain to allow them to be described as chapters … so the numbers (well, titles, because it looks better – are you getting the gist of how my literal mind works yet?) (This would be a good time to escape if brackets and ellipses are not your thing!) … anyway ...

So, the titles at the top will indicate the start of a new thought or new 'topic.'

Secondly, this book really won't read like any other book you have read … The reason it has taken so long to write is that I've been trying to do it the standard book way. However, my brain simply does not function that way, and I'd bore you to tears if I tried to push through and write it like that.

It won't have chapters and headings, and it will jump between I, we, they, and you because that is the way my brain operates (thank you, ADHD) … The context will ensure it is always clear and make it flow far more naturally.

Some bits may feel a little long-winded, and it will be clear that I am writing more detail than my brain wants, so it might feel a little unnatural. Bear with me, those are the bits I feel you really should know, but I haven't managed to condense them into short, catchy snippets yet!

Thirdly, and most importantly, this is a book intended to be one of hope ... a story of not just survival but of true living ... of helping your child have that authentic, wonderous, magical experience of life that I finally have a glimpse of after decades of looking on through the fog. If it leaves you feeling any other way, I demand you email me and ask for your money back immediately.

This is a book about the human mind and relationships; there is nothing within it that cannot apply to every neurotype. Everything within it will help everybody understand themselves and have richer, more fulfilling lives and friendships. However, it is important to remember that while the adjustments are **beneficial for all** ... they are **crucial for some** and can be the difference between flying and drowning.

Beneficial for all; crucial for some.

Prologue

I am writing this book because it simply does not exist.

I am writing this book to bring peace and understanding to your family.

I am writing this book because nobody wrote this book for me or my family.

I am writing this book to save your child's mental health.

I am writing this book to save your child's life.

I am writing this book because what I have learnt has saved my own.

I am writing this book because, for every family I reach, I save 11-year-old me all over again.

There are thousands of parenting books out there … from the deeply therapeutic to the most didactic behaviourist (I'm looking at you, Super Nanny). However, there are still thousands and thousands of families stuck in a parenting vacuum where, at best, the current advice doesn't work; at worst, it is increasingly damaging their own and their children's wellbeing.

We now have a deeper understanding of the impact of our generation's, usually well-intentioned, parenting on the mental health of the nation, if not the world. We have seen suicide rates and the need for treatment for depression and anxiety soar, and we have blamed many aspects of current society for this. While, of course, it plays a part, there is overwhelming evidence that our early childhood experiences have the greatest impact on how we manage in the adult world.

Suicide rates amongst neurodivergent (ND) adults are nine times higher than the national average. The average life expectancy for an autistic or ADHD adult is 49. Deaths are mainly attributed to dying by suicide, but also due to self-medication through drugs, alcohol, food and risky lifestyles in response to a lack of support and understanding.

The number of ND people in prison, youth offending institutions, exclusion units, mental health organisations, and living on the streets is grossly disproportionate to those without ND.

Anxiety and depression are not, I repeat, are NOT part of the diagnostic criteria for being neurodivergent. They are a by-product of growing up and living in a world that is not willing to meet your neurotype halfway. It puts all the pressure on the ND individual to adapt and work against their natural state of being.

All humans have core strengths and barriers. In the majority, neurotypical barriers are already understood, and allowed for, within the world they have created … However, for those not born within that majority, the barriers lead to anxiety because nobody else seems to be struggling to 'do the simple thing' … Then there is guilt about why we are apparently so capable one minute but so incapable the next. (We really do internalise all those words: "You're just not trying hard enough; if only you focused/ weren't so lazy/just got on with it" …) Ultimately, this leads to the most corrosive of emotions – shame, and the cycle of destruction begins.

This book aims to peel back those layers to take you and your child on a journey to celebrating the wonder that is the neurodivergent mind. To portray it as a superpower while it is still causing so much pain is an insult to those who feel broken and powerless. First, we must:

- Understand – What do I/they need? Why? Why has it been so hard?

Then

- Accept – There are barriers and limits, especially in a world not created for a particular neurotype … This is neither good nor bad in itself; it just IS!

Then

- Strategise – Implement practical ways to overcome the barriers and limitations that have been identified.

Very soon

- Life feels a little more manageable ... a little less overwhelming and difficult.

Then

- Thrive – The beautiful by-product of seeing what you are capable of when you are on an equal footing.

NOW you can celebrate ...

Our journey together – A note from the author (well ... me)

Just like most journeys into finding peace, it has to start with why we go searching in the first place.

We set about seeking answers because how we are experiencing life hurts ... very often, the family have reached a breaking point ...

The parents feel powerless, especially as they really have tried everything suggested to no avail ... or even worse ... things are MORE desperate, despite all the "support."

The children are displaying signs of increasing and extreme anxiety ... they've stopped eating, they have shut down, they can't attend school, and they can't even leave the house ... their bedroom ... their bed. They have started melting down alarmingly regularly, and they may be physically hurting themselves or others ...

... they are screaming out, literally, loudly or silently, for help ...

They feel beyond help because they, too, have been subject to all those courses, therapies, tools and strategies ... and things are worse than ever ...

It is usually at this point people reach out to me, just desperate that their child stops hating life and hating themselves ...

Then the healing can begin ... it starts with understanding for everyone: understanding why it all hurts so much. To frame it as a gift at this point is insulting to all involved.

There may be resistance and anger at the notion that who they are is deemed pathological, and a doctor has to give it a name ... I mean, it IS ludicrous that our personality is a diagnosis!

Over time and with support, there is acceptance. Work can then begin in earnest to adjust their world to hurt less and give them the tools to self-accept, regulate and advocate.

Finally ... once they start seeing what they are capable of when the world isn't working against them ... I get that call from a teen who refused even to say autistic a few months ago ...

They say, "How do neurotypicals actually get good at anything without hyperfocus and the dopamine of a new interest?"

And I know they have started to understand and celebrate the beauty of their gift ... their brain ... them. Just them.♀

Why you should read this book

You should read this book because it provides a unique perspective and therapeutic yet practical approach to supporting ND children and families. This perspective is borne of the combination of 48 years of lived experience and 20 years of studying, researching, observing, and supporting the most distressed children.

On my journey through education, I met hundreds of children at a crossroads, where others could see only one clear path for these young people ... I could see very clearly there was an alternative to the hopelessness attributed to their future. I could see that we had a choice. We could continue to 'contain' these children until they were independent and therefore nobody's responsibility but their own ... Alternatively, we could help them understand themselves. We could give them and their families the tools to advocate for their right to take up space, be heard and be accepted for who they are so they could stop fighting themselves and the world.

This book will provide you with an understanding of your child (and very possibly yourself) that will help you overcome your fears and have hope for their future. It will also guide you through practical strategies for helping your distressed child in the middle of a meltdown and show you how to move on, learn from and, over time, diminish the meltdown. This book will restore or save your relationship with your child as well as their relationship with themselves … All of these are excellent reasons why you should read it … But, fundamentally, you should read this book because I believe it could ultimately save your child's life.

Who am I?

The relevant bits for this book are that I am autistic, I have ADHD (Attention Deficit Hyperactivity Disorder) (I'm still looking for an identity-first introduction that sounds better than an ADHD-er and removes the disorder from my identification), and I am also diagnosed with PDA (Pathological Demand Avoidance).

I didn't know all this on that day 11-year-old me came out of school, slumped to the pavement right outside in utter exhaustion, barely registering my bag fall down my arm to the ground. If I had known, I would have understood why I sat there for hours until I was found and taken home. Once there, I promptly broke down, sobbing that I couldn't breathe and that I felt like something was choking me ... I could have explained why shouting at me, demanding to know what had happened that day, as I lay curled up under a duvet, was making me want to sleep and never wake up again.

I tried going back to school after that; I really did ... I tried to use whatever mechanism had allowed me to keep going back, day after day, up to that point, but I couldn't. I never attended a full day of education again. Not school, not college, not university; yet here I am writing this book after becoming a teacher, then a specialist head teacher, then a SENCO and now a business owner. You see, my intelligence and capability were never in question; in fact, they worked against me. I was able to find so many ways to hide my difficulties and achieve academically, keeping me just enough below the radar that people didn't notice the scars from rubbing the chain against my skin until it cut the surface. They didn't notice the effect of the vodka that went from being a rare reprieve to a crucial survival tool by the time I was 13, and because nobody understood, least of all me ... they didn't seem to care.

One marriage, two breakdowns, a bout of homelessness, a string of jobs and broken relationships, hundreds of pills later ... I discovered the truth; I am not broken, untreatable, or unlovable. I am autistic; I have ADHD and PDA. That's it.

Who are the children?

They are the children who cannot comply. Even when they really, really want to … even when they have chosen 'the thing' … BEGGED for the thing; then suddenly, the weight of expectation appears to render them incapacitated.

Some of them have labels; in fact, all of them have labels! It's just that some are given by doctors and psychiatrists, while others are slapped on by society.

At some point in our evolution, somebody decided to box up 'normal' based on the traits, strengths and limitations of the vast majority. Those that did not fit the box were then deemed broken, deficient, and given a label; autistic, ADHD, anxious, selfish, sociopathic, egocentric, disruptive, stubborn, naughty, and feral … to name a few.

But they are not deficient; they are wired up differently. Wired up to never forget that we are all born free and that we have everything we need to thrive in this world … if only we did not become drowned out and worn down by arbitrary 'shoulds' created by the elusive 'they' … if only we are allowed the autonomy, trust, independence and space to do so.

The founding principles

In the following pages, I will outline the founding principles of the *Raising a Wild Child* philosophy and approach to parenting. These principles are true regardless of neurotype, age, social status, race, or gender … They are the foundation of being able to co-regulate and form a mutually authentic, loving and supportive relationship between a parent and child.

They are the phrases and concepts I found myself repeating, time and time again, to support parents and hold them close through the avalanche of opposition, not only from outside sources but from their own fears and traumas. These are the beliefs required to get through this journey with your child to a place where you can feel heard and understood and be your authentic self. These are the foundation of the immense success of the Wild Child approach, and without them, the struggle can only intensify.

They can feel counterintuitive, and some are very difficult to hear as they can evoke fear, trauma, regret and guilt in many adults. Please, be as kind and compassionate to yourselves as possible. This is not a space for reproach or judgement; I promise you. If you have picked up this book and read it this far, you have done the absolute best you could in every moment with the tools you had and the advice you were given. Everything you did came from a place of love for your child ... that is never, ever in doubt.

So, the principles can feel counterintuitive and the exact opposite of every 'should' you have internalised ... Yet if you take a moment and let go of the guilt, the fear and the 'shoulds,' they will feel intuitively and unequivocally true. This philosophy is not meant to teach you anything you don't already know. It is intended to guide you back to what you instinctively know about your child and how you would love to parent them ... if only the world would lean back and give you the space to do so.

The 80/20 ratio

The question, "Aren't we all a bit autistic?" (the answer is no to that, by the way – that's it, "No.") … appears to have been replaced by, "We all have to do things we don't like," "We all have to mask," and "Wouldn't we all like that accommodation?" …

Yes, we all have to mask to a degree … surely we'd mostly turn up to work in pyjamas at midday otherwise. However, when the world is set up to largely accommodate your needs and, at the very least, not actively aggravate them 90% of the time, you can cope with the 10% of required things you don't like and even things that hurt, including injections, getting the flu, etc. …

However, when you feel like you are holding your breath and suffocating in the face of the sensory onslaught and confusion of existing in a world not created with you in mind at all … When you spend all day suppressing your reactions, censoring yourself, being confused, and using every single strategy in your midst to get through … you break! Eventually, you just can't do it anymore. Yes, burnout hits.

By the time families come to our team for family support, their child has done everything within their power to survive, attend school and keep up, and they are exhausted. It is then time to allow them to rest and ensure when they emerge, the adults around them and the environment are set up to meet their needs at least 80% of the time … Dammit, even 70 % will do, but I like to hope.

For a very long time, the child's needs will have to be met 100% of the time as they heal and recover (remember, it's a joint, not a muscle!) … You will know once they start to heal, and you'll know when we can start gently introducing the 20%.

When we see children manage the 20%, it is tempting to think, 'Well, I can use those same strategies to get them to do more … and more … and more.' Then we wonder why we're back to square one … (and then, it's even harder to make them feel safe enough to rest and recharge effectively before trying again).

It takes time to heal years of suppression, masking and trauma … it takes even longer for young people to know what they want or need. They haven't ever been asked, and the last time they tried to get their needs met, it didn't work out too well for them! (you know, the "It's not too hot, you should just listen more." "It's not loud; you just need to try harder," thing they went through) …

So it takes a long time for them to feel safe enough to re-access that part of their brain. It is why we don't ever need to offer solutions again … we just need to ask, "How can I help?" For a long time, you will get nothing, or "I don't know" … We can only apologise to them for not having the answers and convincing their brain that we did know what they needed. Hearing the question, "How can I help?" often and consistently not only wakes up the part of the brain that asks, 'What do I need … what do I need?' It also reminds them that you know and trust that the answer is within them, and they will get to it.

Eventually, you will either get an answer, or you will see a change. We don't need to know why or how … we just need to be there to say, "How can I help?"

Low demand does not mean no demand

Children (actually, all humans) need and unknowingly want boundaries to feel safe … I know what you're thinking. My child is kicking me in the shins – they do not want a boundary!

Firstly, I would like to caveat this with when we are discussing setting boundaries with our wild children (or all children, if I'm honest … actually, all humans): we must choose boundaries that are rational, logical and worthwhile.

As part of the 'lean back' conversation I have with parents, I ask them to examine the rules they feel are important. What are the non-negotiables that feel really important to them? … Then, we decimate them. ☺

Why is something a rule? What 'should' have you absorbed? What are you afraid of if this rule is not followed?

I often relay the story of when I was discussing the rule 'we must all sit around the table for dinner' with a parent. Their response was it is important as it is the only opportunity to bond as a family. They were afraid that if it didn't happen, then the family would be fragmented, and nobody would have a chance to share what was happening in their world … All of this was said very loudly in order to be heard over the screaming and plate smashing I could hear in the background … it didn't sound very bonding.

So … is it sharing information and bonding that you are craving, or sitting around a table?

This family agreed to meet for ice cream every day, sprawled all over the living room.

The other example is the fresh air and exercise rule …

Me: So why do they need to come to the park with you?

Parent: Because they need fresh air and exercise.

Me: Why can't they open a window and do star jumps?

Parent: …

Me: …

Parent … (They actually asked if I was secretly their child as that's exactly what their child would say.)

Me: So why DO they have to come to the park?

Parent: I want them to.

Me: Why?

Parent: Because I miss doing things as a family, and I love this particular park and want to share it with them. (It took a few whys to get here ... but even I can't put you through that, regardless of how helpful it would be for the word count!)

Me: Then tell them that. Let them know the real reason and let them know they are not obliged. Tell them you'd love for them to come, but completely understand if it's too much. Ask them if there is anything you can do that makes it more possible for them.

It is crucial that children know there is no consequence if they don't make it, not even your disappointment ... I know it is counterintuitive, and I can't promise it will mean they will go. I do promise that it will make it far more likely and won't add to the shame and anxiety.

Anyway, back to being kicked in the shins ...

You have decided that this is a crucial and fair rule. You have provided the 80/20 ratio that makes it more likely ... you set the boundary ...

And they push back HARD ...

What is happening here is that all humans will push against a boundary to find out one of two things ...

1) Will you change the boundary? In this case, you are afraid of me, which means you cannot keep me safe = anxiety and behaviour through the roof.

2) Will you retaliate in anger, rejection (even an eye roll is seen as rejection when you feel this unloveable), or in any other threatening manner? Then I am scared of you as you cannot keep me emotionally safe = anxiety and behaviour through the roof.

That is why the key is to remain as lovingly present as possible while standing your ground. The consequence is the way they are feeling. No other consequence is required for future learning about boundary-pushing. For example, a child who has missed out on their favourite food and won't have an available alternative because they threw it away … in the time before they have access to the food again, they will complain and demand you make it available.

Tempting response: What do you expect? Have you learnt your lesson? You shouldn't have thrown it away …

Healing response: I know, it's so frustrating when our brain makes choices that mean we lose what we like … Shall we see if there is anything else you like, or shall we play a game while we wait for a replacement?

You do not have to break the boundary by going out and getting the food at all costs, but you don't have to be angry about it either.

Note:

A useful phrase when they are really pushing and saying, "Just do it. Why don't you just do it?" is "I love you too much to teach your brain that this is how we get what we want" **and/or** "I'm sorry I won't take the easy way out and teach your anxiety that it can make you and me do unhelpful things."

Child of today

You are parenting the child of today, not the adult of tomorrow

The above says it all, in those moments when your anxiety joins their anxiety and your mind is propelling you into the future where your child ends up alone, in prison, being assaulted, missing their lesson, excluded, homeless, jobless …

Please know that the outcome you are most afraid of is far more likely if you try to fix it right then and there and join in the chaos … I cannot promise that the bad thing won't happen. I can promise that it is less likely to, and you will all cope much better with it if we stop adding anxiety and energy to the scenario playing out in front of you.

I promise, meeting chaos, anger, anxiety, and fear with calm does not mean you are making a rod for your own back or setting a precedent … and it certainly does not mean they are 'getting away with it' …

… Lean back, breathe, and take a look at your child … Getting away with what? That feeling you are seeing is consequence enough.

You have one job

You have one single job as a parent … love your children

That's right … unconditionally, unequivocally and unwaveringly.

It is not our job to educate them or make sure they learn what they are told to.

Or to make sure they have friends.

Or that they have a well-paid job when they grow up.

Or even 'meet their potential' through our eyes.

It is most definitely not our job to shield or distract them from their feelings … any of them. Disappointment, anger, happiness, sadness, fear … Nope, it's not our job to take any of those away.

Through the moments when we look at them in awe and the moments that we are utterly flummoxed as to why they can't do 'the simple thing.' Through the exclusive diet of the plainest Tesco pasta (other brands are available … No, no, don't buy another brand if your child said Tesco … they WILL know!) and the sharpest pickle known to humankind. Through the disappointment that looks so crushing. Through the confusion when they decide their friends don't like them anymore, and through the collection of seemingly identical rocks. Through the rage, the seemingly unbearable anxiety, and through the 843rd rendition of We Don't Talk About Bruno, through the monologue about the galaxy and all its stars … and through the disagreements, the rage and the sadness that follows …

One job … don't try and fix; just love them. That's really it. Try it and see what happens.

So next time you doubt your ability as a parent or if you wonder if you have done 'enough,' refer to this page and the 'to-do' list below. If you can tick that box … superb! You've passed.

Perfect parent to-do list	Tick when complete
Love the child/ren unconditionally through it all	

Our children don't owe us a single thing

I've said it before, and I'll say it again ... it is a fortunate quirk of nature that our children seek our love and approval.

Accepting that we have no automatic authority or right over them is crucial for preserving the relationship, especially if they are one of the wonderous wild children.

We talk about compromise in relationships, and sure ... in peer-to-peer relationships, each party has the free will (I know I am simplifying this and not accounting for abuse/trauma/practicalities for the sake of this example) to decide whether they can accommodate the other person's needs and the level to which they can do so without hurting themselves emotionally. Nobody can move too far out of their comfort zone for prolonged periods as resentment and a loss of self creeps in (this is why the current model for marriage counselling is so unsuccessful long term – a story for another day or another book maybe: if I ever get this one written!).

Anyway, in peer-to-peer relationships; we are choosing to be there … In the parent-child relationship, only one person signed the contract! Sure, you may not have read the small print that you may get a wild one that will overturn every notion you had about parenting to that point … but you signed the contract; they didn't.

They did not ask to be born; they did not ask us (parents) to make sacrifices. They did not ask us to stay up all night worrying about them ... we chose to do all of that ...

... so, they don't owe us a single thing. Nope, not respect or compliance or fulfilling their potential or being happy or grateful … nada; not a thing.

This does not mean that your needs as a parent do not matter at all, but it does mean you cannot look to your child to fulfil your dreams and wishes. You will need a network of support and understanding to cradle you through the 'catch them if they fall' parenting that a successful relationship with a wild child requires. You will also need to understand your own triggers and needs and ensure you are compassionate and kind to yourself. Everybody needs to feel okay and be able to set boundaries around their own wellbeing … The parent just has to move further out of the comfort zone that feels safe for them because … you know … the one-sided contract.

Children tell us

Parents often come to me in complete surprise that their previously seemingly calm and coping child is suddenly having explosive meltdowns. It feels like it has come completely out of the blue, that the trigger is arbitrary, if even obvious, and that there is no reasoning at all.

To add to the confusion, their child seems beyond fine, happy, in fact, with other people or during the activity they had 'violently' resisted moments before.

The truth is, this isn't sudden ... children tell us. They tell us they are distressed; we just don't understand the language. First, they tell us with words, "I don't want to go to school/football/the party*") and we are surprised. They love school/football/parties while they are there; in fact, they even pestered to go.

It must be an off day, so we say, "Oh, don't be silly. You love it there ... come on," and we cajole them out of the door.

All the way there, they are thinking, 'I do love it, I am happy ... There's just this feeling ... this feeling ... ummm... I don't actually know what this feeling is; I must be imagining it ... Yes, I love it. It's fine. I just need to cheer up, try harder … ignore that feeling; it's in my head. But there it is, every time … it's not going away; it's getting stronger …'

So they tell us again, this time by delaying walking out of the door, taking hours over breakfast, and losing their socks. "No, not those socks … the other socks. Where's my bag? I just need the toilet. Yes, again …"

… and we encourage and cajole again. "It's okay. You know you love it when you're there."

So we pull on our socks, grab a cereal bar for breakfast on the way and off we go again …

'But that feeling … it's getting bigger, I can't concentrate at school, and I feel so tired after school … that feeling …'

So, they tell us again. Now they are rooted to the ground; they're holding onto the door frame, refusing to get dressed …

… we're in a rush to get to work. 'This is just silly now,' we think. 'They still seem absolutely fine, MORE than fine, when they are there. They are becoming so controlling over everything, and now they think they can control this.' We pick them up. "Come on, you're fine. Let's go."

'I am not fine …' they think.

'I am not fine ... that feeling.'

'But it doesn't make sense. I don't know what it is; nobody else sees or feels it. Everybody else just gets on with what they have to do; they finish everything they are asked to do.

It must be me. They're all right ... I just don't try hard enough ... I must be stupid; I must be lazy.'

'I am bad. My poor parents are getting angry because they need to get to work; they've paid for this football ... "Hang on," they say. "You ASKED for the football, begged in fact."'

'What is wrong with me? I must be broken. I need to hide this; I am horrible. I just need to try harder.'

'But that feeling ...'

Then they tell us by hurting themselves or others ... by screaming, shouting, hitting, crying, withdrawing, shutting down, throwing.

Then we listen.

We have no choice; we simply can't get them out of the door.

Then their brain goes, 'Oh, okay. THAT's what I am meant to do when something feels wrong ... That's how people help.'

...

Our job is to peel back that anxiety, guilt and shame ... roll it all the way back and listen when they tell us with their voices.

To believe them, validate the feeling and ask how we can help, even though, for a long time, they will respond with "I don't know ..."

We pause, and we thank them for telling us. We promise we are going to help them work out what feels bad and look for ways together to understand and try to make it feel easier ...

I have a theory

I have a theory ...

At a certain point in our evolution, 'they' boxed up normal and created a system to produce a compliant, efficient, predictable, and measurable workforce.

Anybody not fitting that box was pathologised and given a label to make them feel inferior and broken ... leading to compliance and dependency, if not efficiency.

Either way, you've subdued the vast majority.

I do not view being autistic or ADHD as a disability. We communicate and experience the world differently through our senses and thought processes ... when celebrated and harnessed, it can produce brilliance.

So, "What is the difference between those inside and those outside of the box?" I hear you ask ... Well, I'll pretend you asked exactly that because I'd like to give you the answer I have come to after over 20 years of working with groups of people, conducting extensive research and my own lived experience.

Fundamentally, I believe that every human on earth wants to belong, to have a tribe, to connect and be part of a group … Every human also wants and needs autonomy, to live authentically, to call out and fight injustice and to be heard.

For those inside the box (referred to as neurotypicals (NTs) for the sake of clarity and in the absence of a more useful definition), their need to fit in and belong is slightly greater than their need to speak out and chase what they believe is 'right' at all costs.

For those outside the box (neurodivergents (NDs) … although I have coined the term neurodifferent recently, I like it … I might keep it – I'll keep you posted), well, for us NDs, the need to be autonomous, authentic and call out injustice is slightly greater than the need to belong.

That's it, really; there is no superior or inferior way to be … there just happen to be more people inside the box.

Let me tell you a story that illustrates this …

When I was a teacher, I would hear the grumbles in the staff room about an injustice or something really making everybody miserable … my ND radar goes on; there is a problem … must fix said problem. How do I fix the problem? Well, go to the decision-makers, of course … Remember, we have no sense of hierarchy and status … So off I pootle to the headteacher to fix the injustice …

Now … EVERYONE is angry at me!

Apparently, I should not have gone to the headteacher and 'snitched' that they were all unhappy (it would seem that NTs bond by having a shared problem; they didn't want an actual solution! This makes zero sense to my 'accept or change things' brain!) … so **they** were mad at me.

The headteacher wasn't pleased either … but bless her. Apparently, it wasn't her fault; it was the head of children's services who was the barrier … you guessed it … where did I tootle off to next? Yeah … it didn't end well, and I found myself embroiled in a whistleblowing allegation, genuinely baffled as to how I got there!

And that is how we end up alienating ourselves time and time again … would I do things differently next time? I so wish I could say "Yes." I wish I could just keep my head down and blend … but, sorry … it's a compulsion.

The compulsion to fix and call out unfairness will always outweigh the need to belong … whereas for my colleagues … their compulsion to belong will always matter more than fixing things. I guess that's how the world balances out!

Lean back … a bit more … bit further …

The most difficult conversation I have with parents, the one that frightens them the most, is the 'lean back' conversation. It's the one where I have to draw their attention to the fact that they can't 'make' their child do anything. You see, the born free child doesn't buy into the idea of automatic authority or hierarchy (society did make up these concepts, after all) … Someone being older or choosing to give birth to them does not mean they have to comply unquestioningly with their requests.

It is a fortunate quirk of nature that our children generally want our love and approval, so they do try to appease us. It is this going against their innate nature that creates the anxiety around demand avoidance and demand paralysis.

The internal battle between wanting to please our caregivers and the resistance to being controlled, coerced and treated as though everything we do is 'because you said so' really undermines our sense of self and feels like constant humiliation. This is also why we react to praise as well as negative consequences.

It is so counterintuitive. As parents and carers, we feel we must DO something to help. It goes against all our natural instincts that our job is not to protect our children from anger, fear, disappointment, or 'failure' ... it is to cradle them through all of those emotions and the actions that led to these outcomes.

This is the only way to free them to try everything and take risks without always worrying that they will hear, "I told you so." "What did you expect?" "See, you should have listened to me; I knew this would happen." "You caused this. Why are you angry?" ...

I'm sorry we (the royal one referring to the demand 'avoiders') only ever learn 'the hard way.' No amount of telling us makes sense, as we can't visualise or feel words. We do not process words; we process experience ... If every experience ends with, "Interesting. What have we learnt? What next?" then we are going to do a whole lot more ... It will mean we will be far less anxious as we aren't grappling with your disappointment in us on top of our failure and the judgement of others.

"But even with me reminding and 'nagging,' they barely do anything ... they'll do NOTHING if I leave them to it!" I hear you cry ...

Nope, this is the root of 'demand avoidance' ... We are not resisting you. We are fighting for the autonomy, independence and trust in our intrinsic motivation and strength that we know we are born with ... It just takes lots of time, patience and courage from everyone while we re-find it.

That's right, the less we are asked to do, and the less invested you are in us doing/succeeding at it, the more we can do!

"Belonging is being part of something bigger than yourself.

But it's also the courage to stand alone and to belong to yourself above all else."

Brene Brown

It is such a shame

No, not your child's neurotype … the shame that the world creates in response to it; for you as well as your child!

The shame that is created when your child and, consequently, your whole family do not meet the expectations of the social and educational systems that surround you – The … dun dun duuun … **NORM.**

We shall explore the concept of 'normal' or 'the norm' or 'typical' further on in this segment … for now, let's discuss what we are doing here.

Raising a Wild Child was borne of my own shame, or, to be more accurate, the *healing* from my own shame …

I have spent my life embarrassed and ashamed that I did not blend in, that I just couldn't get life 'right,' and that I couldn't do the 'simplest' things … Somewhere deep down (very, very, very deep down), I knew that I was an intelligent being. I thought things that other people didn't, I noticed things others didn't, I figured things out in a way that they couldn't … but I couldn't tie my shoelaces (still can't … they are so fiddly and boring, dammit) … So although I would go on to be found to have an IQ of 147, nobody was assessing me on all those amazing things I could do. They were just judging me on the fact that I couldn't tie my own shoelaces … Now, replace shoelaces with a myriad of other mundane (to me, at least) tasks that I could never master over the course of my education. You can see how I would have a really corroded sense of self and feel like anything I did know was of no value. In fact, it often got me into trouble for being a show-off, off-task, irritating, a know-it-all. However, the only thing that mattered when it came to measuring my value as a person was those damn shoelaces …

So, I began hiding everything I struggled with. I became distraught if ever I slipped up and showed a weakness – hence our apparent 'perfectionism.' It turns out it's just a crippling shame and fear of failure!

So I hid both my struggles and my strengths … basically, I hid all of me.

The struggle to keep still.

The struggle to follow instructions.

The struggle to learn anything I wasn't interested in.

The struggle to understand why people did or didn't like me.

The struggle to initiate conversation.

The struggle to find my way from the lunch hall to the playground.

The struggle not to burst into tears whenever the loud bell went.

The struggle not to melt down in a heap of screams after that day's 5th unexpected change.

The struggle to tie my blinking shoelaces!!!

I hid it all, and I watched intently for every clue from others and the environment to ensure I wasn't going to 'mess up' … I was pretty sure I was hiding it all really well … I didn't stand out … I fit in. But, I remember the deep loneliness as I looked across enviously at my classmates that all seemed to just 'know.' I didn't feel like a minority; I felt alone.

Alone and ashamed.

Yes, I fit in, but I did not belong.

The ultimate aim of *Raising a Wild Child* is to diminish shame. Shame destroys all relationships … the one we have with ourselves as well as the ones we have with others.

Shame comes on gradually. First, you develop a layer of **anxiety** around your 'inability' (What's wrong with me? Why can't I do what others can? Why do they find it so easy and I'm so confused?) …

… Then the **guilt** sets in (I should just try harder, I'm lazy, I should focus, I'm embarrassing others, I'm letting everyone down) …

Then the **shame** comes (I must hide this in any way I can, overcompensate, laugh at myself when I'm hurting, never show weakness, never show vulnerability … nobody must ever find out) …

Our job is to peel back those layers … to understand ourselves in order to repair our relationship with ourselves … Once we understand ourselves and look at our struggles and strengths objectively, we can find strategies and solutions.

Once we have a strategy, life feels a little bit easier … If life is easier, we do more, we accomplish more… we believe in ourselves more … Only then can we truly thrive.

'Just' is a powerful word

'Just' … four simple letters in one little word. But it can make us feel so small, so insignificant, just so … nothing.

If it was 'just' that easy, or 'just' a blanket/car/small bit of tomato,* we wouldn't be feeling like our world may end.

We are intelligent, rational human beings … it 'just' really, really matters to us … It's our comfort, our predictability in a scary word, our sensory overload, but you are dismissing it …

Teaching us to dismiss our own discomfort … not teaching us to set safe personal boundaries or about self-care, is why we end up in abusive relationships and why our life expectancy is so low.

… because what if we're 'just' being sensitive, silly, selfish, and they're not manipulative, controlling, coercive or abusive … (relationships)?

What if we're just being silly, and it's not a serious illness … (health)?

What if we're just being silly, and it's not a heartbreaking loss … (emotional healing)?

What if we are 'just' oversensitive and silly ... not deserving of help, and taking up space (loss of trust and validity of our own feelings)?

We don't need to understand why somebody needs something in order to respect it.

If it doesn't hurt the individual or others ... then why not 'just' validate and respect its importance to your child?

*(comforter/interest/sensory nightmare)

It's okay to want to control the world

What would you do if you could control everything and everyone? Wouldn't it be great to be in charge of EVERYTHING??? ... Go on, be honest ...

We know we can't control it all; that's why we can be so frustrated so often ... yet it doesn't diminish the desire to want it.

But then imagine constantly being told that your natural instincts and way of being are something to be ashamed of, something unnatural, a sign of not being a good person ...

Whether it's your desire to control, to hyperfocus, to move about, to question everything, to need time alone, to speak directly, to create order, to line things up, to sort things, to stim ... simply to exist in your natural state ...

The way you play, the way you think, the way you speak, the way you learn, the way you socialise, the way you understand, your very being ... it's all wrong.

It's all wrong and must be hidden at all costs ... Imagine what that does to a person's sense of sense and self-esteem? It is no surprise that anxiety and low self-esteem have become synonymous with neurodivergence.

It's really okay to WANT to control the world ... toy with that idea. "What would you make your teacher do? What would you do to your bedroom? Ahhhh, wouldn't that be amazing???" Then agree, it's a shame we can't. That is a very different message that may just save a child's mental wellbeing.

We all need our feelings

It would seem that at some point in our evolution, we decided to put a value judgement on feelings. We decided that we must only ever feel one emotion … happy. My suspicion is that this coincided with the creation of marketing in its earliest forms. "Ooooh, you don't feel happy… you MUST feel happy … Guess what you need to be happy? … That's right! My thingmabob – happiness can be all yours for three rocks and a Flintstone coin!"

You buy the thingmabob and get a temporary boost from having a new shiny thing and the promise of happy … but then it passes … 'Quick! I need another thingmabob (I will stop writing thingmabob soon, promise) … I need happy. I have been told that everybody needs happy, and they are buying the thingmabob. I'll be left out and the only one that isn't happy! …'

Here is what they don't tell you … the feeling was going to pass anyway! AND … here's the most momentous bit … you NEED the other feelings too!

If we were never angry, we would never know when our safety boundary has been crossed. If we were never disappointed, we would never know what was important to us. If we were never excited/anxious (we'll get onto that) ... we'd never have the impetus to get things done.

Imagine you are on an online call, and the internet keeps breaking up ... you get frustrated and anxious, right? Without that frustration and anxiety, you wouldn't do anything about it. You wouldn't do the well-known fix-all (switch off ... back on again ... ta-da), you wouldn't change the location of yourself or the modem, and you wouldn't call the internet company and hold them accountable if the issue persisted ... You'd just sit and stare inanely at the screen until something happened.

Our feelings cannot hurt us! Only our thoughts about our feelings can cause any damage. The only way for feelings to pass is just to feel them. Feeling them is the only way to know if there is a message to be acted upon; feeling them is the only way you can be freed of them, and they can be free to pass. Observe them, move into them by bringing yourself into the present and noticing how they are manifesting in your body (there's a story about this that I'll add at the end. Otherwise, I just take you on the rollercoaster that is my brain and this segment will never finish) ... In the moment, the cause is irrelevant, and trying to figure it out will only complicate things and obscure your thinking. Feel them, let them pass, and then you'll be able to hear their message and call to action if there is one.

The relevance of this to our children is that they need their feelings too. Their feelings cannot hurt them either. I am so often told by young people, and from my own experience ... it is the impact on others of what we feel or do that ends up paralysing us and traps us in the uphill cycle of frustration and anxiety.

Imagine you are driving a car, and you have a 'near miss' ... you would feel anxious, maybe a little frustrated with yourself or the other driver, self-critical perhaps; you may even need to pull over for a while to gather yourself. Then, eventually, it passes, and there is a relief that everybody is okay and the journey can go on ... Now, imagine that same incident, but this time you have a nervous passenger who cares about you (and their own life) very much. Suddenly, there is so much more anxiety, fear of criticism and judgement ... THEN, they say, "Be careful ... you are always so reckless ... I knew you weren't safe on the road," etc. ... Can you feel your 'big feelings' rising even just reading it? What emotions does it evoke? ... Annoyance? Frustration? Self-deprecation? Guilt? Anxiety? Shame? ... None of those corrosive feelings needed to happen if only the person next to you just stayed calm and allowed you to feel your own emotions without comment, panic or judgement. Is it starting to resonate? (if yes, ignore the next paragraph and move on to the story at the end – no, I haven't forgotten!)

No idea what I'm getting at? Well, you know when your child is stuck and can't get out of the door to the thing that they asked for, BEGGED for ... There is nothing you can say to them that they are not already screaming in their own head. 'You asked for this. What is wrong with you? Why do you ruin everything? Why can't you just get up and do it? You're wasting money again ...' WE DON'T KNOW, and saying/shouting the same thing at us is really not going to help us think clearly enough to know what to do next. Staying calm, staying lovingly present (I really must patent that phrase, shush brain ... we can't go and research patents now – see what my brain does???), so ... staying calm, staying lovingly present is the quickest, kindest way to allow that feeling to pass and allow the possibility of finding a resolution. Our feelings cannot hurt us ... Making us responsible for your feelings about our feelings can ...

The promised story

Well, more of an anecdote, really; now I feel like I've hyped it up ... anyway, here it is ...

I had a client come to me, terrified of feeling their feelings. It was painful to watch that feeling try and break through the invisible shield they had created to keep all those feelings in. They woke up every morning with that horrid whole-body anxiety that made them feel sick with fear and trepidation. They would be so afraid of that feeling, they'd try and rationalise it or run away from it – only causing it to escalate and block them from getting out of bed … I asked them to forget about figuring out why they felt that way and how they could fix it. I suggested they move into the feeling, find it physically in their body and imagine describing it to me the next time we speak.

I then received this text. 'It is pointless trying to move into the anxiety … I start to notice it in my arms and legs, then when I try and move into it and describe it … it just disappears, so I can't describe it any more.' … Well, there you go. ☺

We need our children to be okay

Okay, brace yourself ... this may be difficult to hear. We need children to be okay, or at least look okay, more for our own anxiety and wellbeing than theirs.

Let's let that sink in for a moment ...

Ready for the next bit? We are often more willing to accept them **looking** okay ... than actually **being** okay.

I don't blame you! When you know that your child is hurting, you not only feel powerless to take that pain away, but you also feel as though this is somehow your fault. It's what all the professionals are saying ... You need to be firmer, stricter, softer, calmer, do more for them, do less for them, make them come to school, make them do the homework, don't allow them to "dictate their life experience" (genuine quote from a meeting with a headteacher) ... When none of that works and you are still getting blamed and have fingers pointed at you, the last thing you feel confident about doing is turning your back on all that 'support' and taking sole responsibility for your child's welfare. These are trained professionals; are you really going to move the accountability from their shoulders to yours when faced with the downward mental health spiral?

It's frightening, nay ... terrifying, to stand in the face of all that and take the judgement and criticism. I have openly admitted, halfway through the journey with the families I work with, that I hold on with trepidation to a voice screaming in my head. As things appear worse before they get better, it yells, "What if you're wrong? What if **this time** it doesn't work?" ... Emotions that have been suppressed are only released via the occasional explosive meltdown or cut on the stomach where no one can see ... When those emotions start surfacing, and the feelings are given permission to expose themselves, I hold tight, also scared ... but I've never seen it not work ... I have never seen a more pained child once the emotions have been spent, and the pattern settles into the normal ebbs and flows of intense feeling that neurodivergence brings.* It may not look like the family life or education that you envisioned ... but it is a healthier one. Yet riding that wave is lonely, isolating and terrifying ...

This is why we would almost prefer them just to keep that mask on a little longer, cope a little longer, attend a little longer, keep up appearances a little longer ... because otherwise, the spotlight is entirely on you. That is terrifying, and that is when you must remind yourself… you have one single job. Love them. And you do that beautifully.

*Neurodivergents feel things intensely. The natural pattern we expect is from 0-100, then 100-0, with periods of peace and contentment in between. The constant rumbling of anxiety and adrenaline that has you walking on eggshells is, in fact, overwhelm, resulting from masking and unmet needs.

We are not broken neurotypicals …

(It's not us … it's the system)

The system is the schools, the normalised working patterns, and the arbitrary rules … I'm not saying they are wrong, per se … but they are most certainly wrong for us … rendering us disabled when in reality, in the right context, we are really rather able.

For this notion to sit well, we must first discuss the 'diagnosis' thing. I am not saying, in the current climate, that diagnosis is not crucial for validation and support … But I would love to live in a world where the 'label' isn't necessary. Where everybody just meets everybody else where they are at, with compassion and understanding … Regrettably, we don't live in that world yet, so please get the diagnosis if you are fortunate enough to be able to!

However, the fact is, one can be neurotypical and have a learning delay, they can be neurotypical and have mobility issues, they can be neurotypical and have a myriad of other co-existing conditions … BUT the minute one is diagnosed autistic in particular; everything is then brought under that umbrella. This can result in a lot of misunderstanding and, sadly, stigma around what being autistic means. It leads to missed diagnosis and, more tragically, a rejection of young people of their own neurotype as they do not identify with others with the same 'label' (this really perpetuates the loneliness and alienation as you feel like you don't belong ANYWHERE!) … I always start by telling young people how strange it feels to me that fundamentally who I am is deemed a pathological medical condition.

Being neurodivergent, as opposed to neurotypical, basically boils down to two things: the way we communicate and process information and the way we experience the world through our senses. These ways are not inferior; they are just different … and when they set up the working world, they set it up for the majority's needs. So NTs have needs as much as NDs … their needs have just already been catered for (e.g. the need for pleasantries, the need for authority to pass responsibility onto, the need for traditions to create a sense of belonging, etc.). We just need something different; we need to rediscover what that is, and then we need to ask for it respectfully (remember … one rule – don't hurt others or yourself).

In reality, many of the 'problems' neurodivergents face are due to the fact that neurotypicals are more focused on **how** people say things than on **what** they are actually saying ... so more focus is on tone and hidden meanings than on the words themselves.

Bear with me ... let's look at the most common neurodivergent labels:

Autism

Rational, logical, efficient, fair, just, straightforward, attention and commitment to detail and logical empathy are all overshadowed because, by NT standards, we're not fluffy enough in our interactions.

Dyslexia

Dyslexics' brilliant, creative and analytical thinking is overshadowed by a spelling 'mistake.' Please remember we only recently (in historical terms) standardised spelling and grammar. Suddenly human intelligence and value became dependent on remembering spelling and grammar rules, completely detracting from the vast spectrum of skills that make up dyslexic thinking.

ADHD

Incredible connectivity in the brain, attention to detail, commitment to finding the truth, problem-solving, bursts of energy and intense productivity are all overlooked because we forget things or follow the tangents of our brains. We try and fill in every bit of detail for the listener and get loud and passionate when we're in the moment.

In a world that only measures and criticises how we remember and say things and completely ignores what we DO know, is it any wonder we end up with such a poor sense of self, low self-esteem and anxiety?

So, we are not broken neurotypicals … we're just wired differently! As a young man and I concluded recently, there are two operating systems: Mac and Windows … You can use some Windows programmes on a Mac and vice versa. They would sort of work for a while … but then they would start to glitch. The glitches would then become worse until, eventually, the whole system crashes.

Rewards are as demanding and pressuring as 'punishments'

There is a little bit more about this in the 'Helpful bits at the end of a book,' but it's so important it's worth going over it twice (I don't think this will come as a surprise to many people who have picked up this book).

Why? Put simply ... because they undermine both our true intrinsic motivation to be the absolute best we can be and our desire for autonomy and independence.

Every human is born to learn as much as possible with the tools they have been given to be the absolute best they can be.

Nobody needs to teach a newborn baby to cry to get their needs met ... Yet, at about six months, we say our first word ... and everyone REJOICES ... giving kisses and cuddles ... Now, the baby is thinking, 'I didn't say that for you... I said it for me ...' Hmmmm.

Now, some babies can overlook that and think ... 'Whatever, I quite like that response ... I'll do it some more ...'

Other babies, on the other hand, don't like the confusion and misunderstanding about their own motivation and would quite like full credit for it! So they tend not to say much or anything for quite a while after that ...

Because suddenly everything we learn and do is seen as a bid to gain a reward ... praise/attention/a sticker ... but we wanted to learn anyway! We wanted to figure it out by ourselves!

... **Now**, we don't want to do it at all! Especially not in front of you or because you 'taught' us! You know when your child says, "I know!!!" when you know full well that they simply can't know … What they are saying is, "I'm working it out; I want to learn it by myself… I want to learn through trial and error without judgement … JUST GIVE ME SOME SPACE! … please!"

I'm sure you all recognise that rush and agitation as one of your children tries to complete a task before being given full instructions, or that life-and-death scenario of needing to be first or do it before you ask … Well, there you go … that's why! Remember, your job isn't to teach them … just lean back and love them.

We (the wild children) have the right (and need) to struggle

When your child is really young (and maybe not so young!) and you see them struggling, you want to alleviate their distress and 'help.' They shrug you away angrily, saying, "I KNOW!!!" even when you know they don't know, and it's blatantly clear from the scene unfolding in front of you that they, in fact, most definitely DO NOT KNOW!

What they mean is, "I want to work it out myself as much as I can ..." Being shown or taught it somehow devalues the skill and the acquisition of the skill for them ... Remember that learning and doing our best is an intrinsic trait and that confusing our motivation can trigger our demand avoidance ... That's why we try and do something before you can give the instructions ... It's why we scream "Stop talking!" as we are figuring something out! We want to know it was ALL OUR WORK, and we want you to know it too! We need credit for what we do achieve, and we hate credit that we do not feel is deserved ...

Anyway, back to the rights of the wild child.

We have a right to be disappointed when things don't turn out as we wanted, and we have a right to want to try them our way anyway … and then try them our way, again and again, as long as it is not hurting or impacting others. This doesn't mean that you have to say yes to them trying fencing classes for the 346th time even though they have never managed to complete the sessions … It does mean you need to allow your child to request things without making them feel ashamed or reminded of all the times they have 'failed' at seeing them through. They wouldn't be asking if they didn't think they have thought of a way they can manage them and truly believe this time is different … Let me give you an example of how we set the boundary here …

A family has a finite amount of money to spend on after-school care for their child, and they really need the child to be looked after as they have to work. The child is adamant that they want to go to tennis club after school as after-school care … The parents are concerned that they will not manage to make it to the club, leaving them out of pocket and without after-school care.

Tempting Response: *"You always say you'll go, and you never do; I don't trust you to go. You promised last time that you would, but I had to leave work and got into so much trouble. You never see things through, so why should I believe you this time?"*

Alternative Response: *"I can see that you have really thought about this and really want to try again. I am so sorry that I can't afford the lessons **and** the backup plan in case you can't go. This time I have to use the money for someone to be here for you after school, but let's see what we can do about tennis lessons that we can afford."* **Then cradle them through their frustration and disappointment (at themselves and the situation).**

It is always worth remembering that you should only pay and book things if you are comfortable 'losing' the time and money you have dedicated to it ... You, being resigned to the fact that the 'thing' may not happen and the money will be gone, will actually increase the chance of them being able to see it through! It is so counterintuitive ... much like most demand avoidance strategies. The less you 'do' to 'fix,' the more likely you are to fix.

In a world where we have become programmed to 'do' something to fix, we need to reframe the 'doing' as 'leaning back' ... You're not doing nothing ... you're leaning back and maximising the chance for success. THAT is the most selfless parental act I can think of ... overriding your own instinct to help, to alleviate, to fix, ignoring that anxiety and guilt of not coaxing or encouraging; just giving your child space to work through their feelings and reactions to the outcomes of their choices. (This is particularly difficult as we are programmed to rise to the call of distress from our offspring … However, this mechanism was meant to rescue our little cubs from imminent death, not from the modern-day 'risks' of being disappointed, not passing an exam, losing friends, etc. The understanding anxiety segment explains this a little more.)

And finally …

We have a right to our feelings, and our feelings cannot hurt us … What can hurt us is worrying about the impact of our struggle, disappointment and feelings on those we love and who love us … What can hurt us is the judgement of those who "told you so" and "just knew that would happen."

Our guilt and shame over impacting others simply because we want to learn freely and autonomously and in our own space and time creates anger and resentment towards the situation and those we love …

The knowledge that the choice we intuitively want to make will create negative feelings in those around us creates anxiety, choice paralysis and the crippling fear of failure that means we stop trying at all …

Our children do not owe us 'success,' 'happiness,' 'pride,' or 'their potential' … These are theirs alone and must be achieved in their own way to their own definition. We don't have to agree with that to respect it.

One rule ... don't intentionally hurt others. That is the only line we need to draw; then, we need to lean back and facilitate.

What do you want for your child? … No, REALLY want?

The hardest question for those that love a wild child can seem the easiest to answer …

"What do you want for your child?"

The answer is invariably … "I want them to be happy …"

But what if their happy looks nothing like yours … nothing like what society tells you is happy and fulfilled …

What if their happy is huge amounts of solitude or a very small circle of others?

What if it's engaging more in books or online?

What if it's getting a job that just about gets food on their table and a roof over their head … not the one that their 'potential' enables them to achieve?

What if their happy is eating the same thing every day?

What if their happy is not visiting new places, meeting new people and doing new things?

What if their happy makes you feel guilty or powerless and redundant?

What if it makes others question your capabilities as a parent or carer?

What do you REALLY want for the child you love?

Conversation with a parent:

Me: What are you afraid of?

Parent: That he will stop going to school.

Me: Why is that important?

Parent: He needs to get an education´.

Me: Why is that important? (yes, I am that annoying!)

Parent: So that he can get a job.

Me: Why is that important? (see, I told you I was!)

Parent: So that he can earn money.

Me: Why is that important?

Parent: (looking rather agitated and puzzled now) So he can be independent.

Me: Why is that important?

Parent: So that he can feed himself.

Me: So, are you afraid that he won't go to school or that he is going to starve to death as an adult?

…

Can you see that our anxiety, which is fed into by every system around us, equates him going to school with him surviving?

Thankfully, we live in a part of the world where people do not generally starve to death … he will find a roof over his head and food on his table somehow … Right now, we need to make sure he is mentally healthy in order to be able to do those all for himself.

This is usually the point I tell parents that academic capability is the least of our worries for our wild children. Not because mental health is more important (it is … but bear with me), but because the wild child's capability and passion for learning is without question … This capability is what has got them this far with the strategies and masks that they have developed all by themselves … but now they are tired. Academic success and mental wellbeing are not mutually exclusive; it is not an either/or … However, I know that academic success follows mental wellness far more frequently than the other way around.

Their innate drive to succeed has got them this far … but they are tired … they need to rest.

And they need to know that they don't have to do it alone anymore … We believe them, and we will do everything we can to make it hurt less.

I have to squeeze in my favourite analogy here … I was speaking to a doctor when it came to me!

It's a joint, not a muscle!

You will hear lots of professionals tell you that if your child does not keep going, they will regress and lose their resilience and skills. They will shrink their world, which will make it more difficult for them to re-integrate … This is traditional psychology and would be true if the overwhelm and fear were imagined and irrational. If you put someone afraid of balloons in a room of balloons for long enough, their brain will begin to accept that balloons are safe because they have not hurt them.

The things that NDs are exposed to on a daily basis are not irrational and harmless, including:

- the sensory onslaught

- the required hypervigilance to understand what is happening

- the suppressed emotion during changes and transitions

- the misunderstandings that they find themselves at the centre of (having no idea how or why)

- the inadvertent microaggressions

- criticism

- gaslighting

They take a tremendous amount of energy and toil to navigate … these skills are not skills that, the more you use them, the more they grow stronger like a muscle … They are more like a joint. If you have used them to their very limits … they need rest to recover and re-engage. Most of all, they need things to be different when they re-emerge from the rest – we'll talk about how in the second segment of this book.

You can't make me … or them, for that matter!

We cannot MAKE children do anything.

Automatic authority, respect and compliance are all an illusion.

There are only three reasons children do what they are told: they want to, they want to please the person asking, or they are too scared not to!

That's it! Through a fortunate quirk of nature, children are born wanting the love and approval of their caregivers. For most children, this need for approval is greater than the need for autonomy, making it easy for them to put aside their own wishes and comply.

For others, their need for autonomy and independence is greater than the need for approval from parents, peers and society in general … these are the wild children.

It gets even more complicated when we realise that even though the wild children are compulsively driven to seek autonomy, they do actually still want love, acceptance and approval from those around them … They often wish they could just comply and 'not cause a fuss.' But their brain won't allow this compliance as it perceives it as a threat to its very existence.

The nearest I have got to explaining demand avoidance to those not driven by it is this. Imagine that you have been burnt with fire ... then somebody asks you to put your hand in a fire after that: your brain will simply not allow you to do it.

Somebody can be encouraging you to, begging you to, threatening you to or bribing you to. You could even be trying to push one hand down into the fire using the other hand, but your brain will not allow you to endanger your existence.

That is how two parts of one brain can work against each other to protect you.

Following the demands of others and of life (yup, even self-imposed demands that have taken away our choice of what to do in that moment) equates to that fire as far as our brains are concerned. A threat to our autonomy is a threat to our very existence ... the more you ask, the higher the threat level.

That is how demands wake up our survival instinct (amygdala) and why demand avoidance is perceived to be an anxiety disorder.

In those moments, we are as confused as you are, on top of thinking there must be something very wrong with me because there seem to be two voices in our heads. That is why I implore you; please stop telling us what we already know …

"You chose to do this." "You're ruining it for everyone." "You always do this." "You just need to focus." "You just need to try harder." …

I promise we are screaming all those things at ourselves in our heads much louder than you when our feet simply won't 'just' (gosh, that word has so much to answer for!) walk out of the door …

You know when we get angry at you for saying them? … The reality is that we're angry at ourselves, as well as confused and scared that we can't actually seem to make our body do 'the thing.'

In those moments, if you are wondering what your child is feeling, notice what they are trying to evoke in you.

As humans, when we don't have the words to describe our feelings, we try and create that feeling in those around us so they will understand.

So please try and listen to the words while hearing the emotion they are trying to communicate.

Listen to the words while hearing the emotion.

ABA is PBS is new ABA is Trauma

Imagine this ... You've spent the whole day working really hard. You're exhausted from having to please a boss who speaks a whole different language to you and negotiating an environment that hits every nerve ... Too loud, too big, too cold, too hot, too small, too bright, too dark ... Whatever it is ...

Then you get home, and there is your favourite book in the world. You pick it up and start reading ... Just as you unwind and relax enough to lose yourself in it ... someone rips it up, tickles you, demands you talk to them, cuddles you, or just makes noises to distract you ... Every time you pick up that book ...

... There they are.

… This is PIVOTING. A technique used to distract autistic people from their own type of play, following their interest or repetitive, self-regulating behaviours, to stop them from 'entering their own world' ...

... This is 'kind' ABA (Applied Behaviour Analysis).

Now imagine that this is seen not only as completely acceptable but also actually as favourable by someone you spend 4 … 6 … 7 … 9 hours a day with. It wasn't always this way. When you first met them, they took time to play alongside you, took an interest in your interests, and let you lead the way ... You loved being with them, and you trusted them. But then, very, very slowly, they start asking you to do things their way. They are really simple things at first. They know you very well at that point, so they know the things you will find easy to comply with ... (ABA term: low probability demand)

So you think, 'No big deal. I can do that. It's only a few minutes. I like them; they really understand me and let me lead as much as I need ...'

Then the demands become harder and for longer periods, meaning more time away from your interests. Also, they are things that just don't feel natural: sitting up, looking at them, playing in a certain way, communicating their way, not asking too many questions, suppressing your urge to move so much, pretending the lights and sounds don't hurt, pretending the socks don't start feeling like they are cutting off your circulation as the day wears on ...

At first, they gave you treats for doing the things they wanted ... then they started ignoring you when you weren't ...

It is so subtle and so slow and shrouded in such a big smile and approval/reward that you're not sure why you feel so uneasy. Yet you suppress all that unease … This is your friend; they like you; they can't be hurting you … But why do you feel uneasy …? Or even worse … eventually, you don't feel anything at all.

Your body doesn't notice the lights and the sounds or that you're not following your interests or not self-regulating … you don't feel any of it anymore. In fact, your whole body and life don't feel real anymore. It's interesting as you look at yourself from the outside, in automatic pilot … but hey, you're not standing out any more … you blend, you fit in, well, your body does … but you? Who are you? Do you even exist anymore?

We do not de-sensitise, we do not get used to things, we do not grow out of our autistic brain – we de-realise and de-personalise. This is a trauma response and a serious mental health condition. But, like I said, it's okay; everyone around you is more comfortable with your existence now.

So as you can see, ABA is a contentious and controversial approach (unless one is autistic, then it is neither of those; it's widely considered as traumatising abuse).

It is one of the most divisive issues between the neurotypical and neurodivergent communities, on par with functioning labels and how to 'label' or define autism.

So, why is there such a huge chasm?

Well, largely because modern advocators of ABA are genuinely well-meaning, compassionate human beings. They believe, "It has moved on hugely from the 1950s," "It is all about reward and far removed from the electric shock therapy its founders advocated," "It helps the child fit in," "It stops repetitive behaviours," "It teaches functional skills and appropriate behaviour" …

So what is the problem?

Fundamentally, ABA defines 'normal' and anything outside of that definition is shameful and must be curbed or eradicated. ABA takes away the coping mechanisms of the individual, forcing them to stop their regulating behaviours (stimming, covering ears, looking away, moving …) by re-enforcing the idea that these behaviours are wrong and, therefore, shameful. On many occasions, these regulating behaviours diminish over time. The child knows that they must internalise whatever they are feeling and ignore their need to move, stim, look away, speak up, ask questions, or make sounds … They must not draw attention to themselves and their differences in any way.

Can you see the problem here? A child taught to ignore their own needs, so they no longer know which needs are legitimate. The need to be safe? The need to ask someone not to abuse them? Is it abuse, or is this 'normal' even though it feels wrong? Is something feeling awful an indication it is wrong, or am I just being 'sensitive?' I must make eye contact even though it hurts, and I can't focus on anything else. I must not stim, ask or call out … I must keep that mask firmly in place.

And right there is the biggest problem of all. ABA makes the world far more pleasant for everyone except the autistic individual. In the short term, they may look happier and calmer; they fit in … it works.

… but for how long? Five years? Ten years? 15, 20, 40 years? Then what? There is only one result … Autistic burnout!

Autistic burnout takes many forms: depression, suicide, violence, breakdown, law-breaking … However, by the time it happens, the individual is usually an adult or teen who "Should know better." It can't be the unmet need causing the behaviour because they have managed to control it this far, so it must be a choice to behave that way. Therefore, they must be punished and held responsible.

Suddenly the impact of ABA is no longer just a problem for the individual but for society as a whole. One just needs to look at how over-represented the neurodivergent community is in crime, suicide, unemployment, and mental health statistics.

It becomes very clear that ABA is merely a system that puts a sticky plaster of shame over neurodivergent traits and creates a mask that one day just becomes far too heavy to keep wearing. As the mask slips, it leaves an adult that no longer knows who they are, what they deserve and what they need.

Life and society already apply huge pressure on us to wear the mask. ABA reinforces that and intensifies the shame and fallout while touting itself as a kind, compassionate, positive re-enforcement programme that just helps children with neurodiversity 'fit in.'

… But PBS (Positive Behaviour Strategies) isn't the same, right?

Wrong!

It is merely ABA's sneaky counterpart that has added the word positive to distract from the word behaviour … and tried to sneak under the radar into schools all over Britain.

Both ABA and PBS are behaviourist ideologies. They do not seek to understand the sensory, regulatory or communication purpose of behaviour … Even when they do know the underlying cause, they do not seek to address or meet the purpose of the behaviour. They encourage exposure and de-sensitisation to the behaviour (in the words of an ABA therapist, "Yes, I accept that the toothbrush feels like it is burning his tongue, but everybody needs to brush their teeth, so he just has to get used to it.") – but remember, we do not de-sensitise, we de-realise.

Autistic Village put it beautifully … if you don't already follow them on Facebook, please do; they are remarkable!

Quoted from Autistic Village: A comment asked for more information about ABA and the issues with it.

This was my response …

Behaviour training works by engaging the survival mechanism.

Make someone feel so unsafe that they will do what keeps you happy in order to regain safety.

The key mechanism for that is through grooming - become friends - establish a strong emotional bond.

Then ask the child to do things for their 'friend.' Easy things (high possibility demands) at first - and look how happy I have made my friend doing what they want. That is a really nice feeling.

Now the therapist asks them to do things that are less comfortable (low probability demands) - because they are things our brain isn't naturally designed to do. We don't want to.

All of a sudden, our friend doesn't like us anymore – they are ignoring us. This feels really unsafe, and we get anxious. The way to safety is by doing the uncomfortable thing. We do it, and our friend is back, all smiles and treats.

It's okay. It was only a bit uncomfortable – worth keeping the friendship for.

And step by step, more and more 'normalising' is asked of us, that deletes who we are and encourages us to perform 24/7 as someone else. Ignoring our own comfort and our own fundamental wellbeing to keep others happy.

We learn we are so unlovable and unacceptable that we have to pretend to be someone else to keep our friend.

And our automatic protective mechanism, our dino brain, learns that fawning – excessive people-pleasing – is the best way to keep us safe.

This means that when the next abuser that comes along, we are easy pickings. We have already been groomed and trained to make the other person happy at the expense of our comfort. This looks like a normal relationship to us.

Behaviourism doesn't look for a cause beyond the basic 'doesn't want to' or 'attention-seeking.'

I don't want to put my hand on a hot stove. The issue isn't me not wanting to harm myself – the issue is the hot stove. Find out the reason for the avoidance and deal with that – then there is nothing to avoid.

In ABA, you are taught to be okay with putting your hand on the hot stove over and over.

And 'attention-seeking' is really 'safety-seeking.' As children, we are highly vulnerable – we rely on those around us to keep us safe and protect us. If they aren't doing that, then we need to get their attention so they will.

The answer is to find out what is causing them to feel unsafe and deal with that. Reassuring them they are protected and safe.

ABA teaches you that, no matter what you do, NO ONE is coming to protect you. There is no point in asking for help or support because none is coming. And if you DO keep asking, then you will get ATTACKED by the person you saw as a protector. So you learn it is NEVER safe to ask for help, protection or support.

Parents see a people-pleasing, compliant child who is no bother. They don't see the terrified fawner who has been emotionally crippled. Unable to trust anyone, unsafe to be themselves, and unable to ask for help if they are in trouble.

ABA is only one 'brand' of behaviourism – the Coca-Cola of behaviourism. All behaviourist techniques are equally toxic and equally under the radar of the observer. And it is prevalent in society.

Hitting children to 'get them in line' was considered 'good parenting' when I was growing up. And we, as a society, have realised that is not okay now.

But we only moved to emotionally 'hitting' children instead. In schools, in many parenting manuals, behaviourism is still everywhere.

Slowly, society is starting to recognise that that is as wrong, if not worse, than physical assault. We aren't there yet, but pioneers like Ross Greene and Mona Delahooke are helping parents recognise that there is a better way.

A way that creates a toolbox of skills for your child to be their happy, authentic self. To build confidence and resilience and support good mental health.

Autistic Village Facebook page

Helpful bits at the end of a book 1

Understanding meltdowns, the crisis cycle and how to respond in the moment

A few crucial things to bear in mind when it comes to anxiety and this whole process

- Anxiety doesn't look or sound like you expect. So, sadly, it doesn't sound like this … "Mother, I have a peculiar feeling in the pit of my stomach and a sense of dread" … It looks more like violence, anger, stubbornness, shutdown, rudeness, insolence, confusion, frustration, or irritability (you get the gist) …

- Anger is a secondary emotion – it cannot exist without a driving emotion: usually overwhelm, confusion, shame, pain, or exhaustion, to name a few.

- Anger is not always loud and outward – your shutdown child will be having all those same emotions that you see in stereotypical meltdowns, just silently and inwards.

- It looks worse before it gets better – remember the 'Children tell us' segment (if not, go back and reread it now). Your child's brain has developed a neural pathway that states 'anger – outward or inward (usually presenting as self-harm, including restrictive eating) is the only way to get your needs met.' What starts out as a purely anxiety-based behaviour becomes an ingrained learned behaviour. However, it is crucial to understand that it is still **not** wilful nor manipulative … your child's brain just hasn't found a better way … yet.

- Once the anger subsides … the emotions will surface. This looks heart-breaking, but it is the only path to healing (remember … we need all our emotions – in this case, it was the warning that there are unmet needs here).

- Anger develops from anxiety because anxiety needs to communicate. Remember the popular adage, 'Behaviour is communication' … this is exactly what it means. During this process, our job is to support the child to believe that we will now listen before anger needs to be used. That anger is no longer required in order to be believed, seen, heard, understood and supported.

- It takes a long time for the body's response to catch up with the brain and feel safe ... You will have to have many conversations and create safety for a very long time before your child's nervous system can believe they are safe and regulate their early signs of anxiety.

- A child who does not have the words or understanding to convey how they are feeling will attempt to create that feeling in their safe person in a bid to evoke empathy and understanding.

- Any human who feels out of control and powerless will feel vulnerable and need to generate a sense and supply of power from others to feel safe (hence the targeting of those perceived weaker or vulnerable.

- Anxious children aren't always aware of how they are coming across and communicating.

- When anxiety is present, the amygdala is awake ... When the amygdala is awake, it believes it is fighting for survival ... so it starts switching off cognition and reasoning. It doesn't want you to think ... it wants you to fight, flight, freeze or fawn. That is why you cannot reason with the awake nervous system. All you can do is co-regulate until it is calm enough to allow reason through.

- This all applies to you, too ... even the pretty picture coming up.

- You need to heal too.

Now for the pretty pictures!

Anybody who has spoken to me for longer than 18 seconds, both in a professional and personal capacity, will be familiar with this picture (I am seriously considering a tattoo of it as I now seem incapable of having a conversation without it).

Stage One: Anxiety/NVS

Your child has come in and seems distressed. Now remember, early signs of anxiety do not look like we expect – so this could look like door slamming, rudeness, or demands. Let me explain.

Context: Your child has just come home from school and slammed a few doors behind them. They come into the kitchen and say (in what appears to be a rude manner):

Child: Why isn't dinner ready? You said it would be ready. You're such a liar!

Tempting response: (because you are human and seriously, what?) You won't get any dinner if you speak like that! How dare you?

While it would seem entirely justified, remember, an anxious child is often unaware of how they are coming across … but we are all human, and if you've just had the most awful day, you may respond in the way outlined above. All this will do is pump more adrenaline into the body, increasing the anxiety and the associated behaviours, which will increase the chance of a meltdown.

The other way

Child: Why isn't dinner ready? You said it would be ready. You're such a liar!

Adult: Ooh,* I don't think you realise how harshly you are saying that. Are you okay?

The chances are you are met with an aggressive 'I'm fine!" and a door slam as they walk out.

If we catch anxiety at this stage, it takes around 15-30 minutes for the adrenaline to drain from the body, and then reasonable conversation can ensue.

 *(Anything that makes you wince and go 'ooh' is usually an anxiety response.)

If, as we are human and have bad days etc. … so we go with response one … more adrenaline is released into the body. The amygdala is even more alert and convinced we are going to die … The amygdala doesn't want you to think; it wants you to fight, flight, freeze or fawn, so it switches off reason, logic and rationale and goes into the anxiety response … This moves the child into **stage two** of the Crisis Arc.

Stage Two: Defensive/Escalation

From stage two, it takes about 45-60 minutes for the adrenaline to seep from the body.

During stages one and two, de-escalation (using the strategies in the de-escalation segment later on) is possible.

If the adult is dysregulated and has persisted with challenging the anxiety head-on, then **stage three** crisis mode ensues.

Stage Three: Crisis

In stage three, there is literally nothing you can do … apart from remaining lovingly present if it is safe to do so.

If you feel regulated enough and safe to stay in the room, then please stay. Position yourself low down next to or behind your child and allow the release of emotions.

It can help you to regulate to view these meltdowns as freeing your child from all the pent-up adrenaline. There is a misconception that a meltdown is harmful or damaging … As somebody who has only allowed myself to go into an outward meltdown a handful of times in my adult life … I can tell you, it is the freest we ever feel.

It is the only time in our lives when we are free from worrying about the impact of our needs and our actions on others … we simply cannot care. And although I have ended up in bed with flu-like symptoms for days, if not weeks, after a meltdown … it is the most cathartic experience in the world.

This does not mean we should be inducing meltdowns, but it does mean that our job is not to suppress that emotion and adrenaline once it has built up … We should take steps over time to stop the build-up, or minimise it and slow it down drastically. The ball of fire is there. We do everything we can to stop it from developing and growing … but once it is there, the kindest thing to do is to free it. Emotions on the outside can be helped … emotions on the inside are the most damaging to their carrier.

For the first few weeks, your inaction in the face of big emotions will appear to cause your child to become angrier … Remember that a child will always push back to see if you will change the rules or react (see the segment 'Low demand does not mean no demand'). Also, remember that we are breaking a neural pathway that we have allowed to develop. We are unteaching that harming yourself or others is the only way to get your needs met.

Stage Four: Recovery

Your child will become very tired. They may fall asleep or go to the ground. We never take a child to the ground, but if it is safe to do so, allow them to lie down. It is the quickest way to 'ground'!

When the cycle has been repeated many, many times, this part can last for hours/days/weeks/months … your child's (we get this too) nervous system has shut down to rest.

Stage Five: Depression

As adrenaline leaves the body, depression hits. This can be harrowing for parents, especially when they hear, "I'm so stupid." "I want to die." "It's too hard." "I will never feel better" … The temptation is to go in with positivity, but all that does is bring to the front of their mind every reason you are wrong! This is where we need to sit with our child, feel and share their energy and validate, validate, validate … not with "But you have so much to be grateful for," or "You are really clever." Instead, try this: "It must be horrible to feel that sad." "I can see how much you are hurting." "I can't imagine how hard you have to try when you feel like this." … You can throw in the odd "I love you" and "It will pass," but both of these can

Crisis Arc

be too painful to hear at this moment, so notice your child's reactions.

Sit with them in their pain. Do you know what? There is an awful lot to be pained about … it **IS** upsetting that the world will end, it **IS** frustrating that people don't care, and it **IS** infuriating that other people won't just do what we want … Validate, validate and validate some more. Remember, your job is not to 'cheer them up' or protect them from their feelings … just sit and love them with everything you have.

After a little while, check in with a connection gesture … "I'm about to start making dinner. Would you like to help?" or "I'm about to make myself a drink. Would you like one?"

This is not the time to discuss behaviour… We are convinced that after each crisis moment or meltdown, THAT is the 'outburst' too far. This is the one that is going to make you hate us, consider us a burden or change the way you feel about us … That is why the connection gesture is **crucial**; it is the ultimate expression of unconditional love. It is the truest "I love you and how I see you has not changed" that we hear, and we need it so much, especially in that moment.

Stage Six: Connection

It is crucial that a reflection takes place only when your child has fully recovered from a crisis.

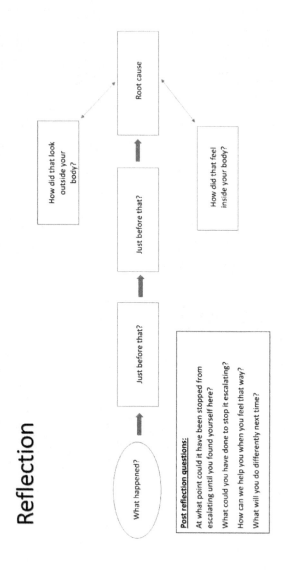

Reflection

What happened?

Just before that?

Just before that?

Just before that?

Root cause

How did that look outside your body?

How did that feel inside your body?

Post reflection questions:

At what point could it have been stopped from escalating until you found yourself here?

What could you have done to stop it escalating?

How can we help you when you feel that way?

What will you do differently next time?

I cannot stress this enough … if your child has been in crisis, it will take at least 90 minutes before the adrenaline leaves their body. Attempting to discuss anything before then will re-activate the nervous system and push your child back into a meltdown.

Parents often say to me, "They woke up in a state, and it has been meltdown after meltdown." The reality is that it was the one meltdown that the child was never allowed the time, space and cradling to recover.

When the time is right (at least 90 minutes later), it is useful to reflect on how you and your child can recognise early signs of dysregulation so that they can de-escalate and/or you can know that it is time to lean back.

The reflective conversation above is a useful template to structure the conversation. Some people like to print this out and write on it; others prefer to use it as a guide for the conversation.

The key is choosing the right moment to ask … "What happened earlier?"

Your child will either get angry that you are discussing a moment they would rather forget (in which case it's too soon … lean back), or they will be tempted to go back to the beginning (well, the part where somebody else was to blame ☺) … So guide them back to the last part … "No, right at the end" …

Child: I hurt Isaac.

Adult (stay soft and reassuring): What was happening just before then?

Child: He said I was rubbish.* (*I am fully aware that their version may be a touch more colourful)

Adult: That can't have felt nice … What was happening before that?

Your child will tell you the "he said, they said, she said …" Let them root back as it helps their memory go back to that moment. This allows them to safely create the somatic body feeling we would like them to recognise as an early sign of escalation.

Often, you will find that this backward chaining goes back further than you realise. It can give you an insight into your child's experience neither of you would have recognised was the actual reason for distress … For example, a child has come in from school. It appears that they are annoyed that you hadn't cooked what they expected, resulting in you becoming upset that you are being criticised.

The backward chain takes your child back to ten minutes before being anywhere near the front door. "Nobody would sit with me on the bus; they called me weird," or "I left school so angry. I've been told off all day long, and I really did not do anything wrong." …

Ensure you validate and soothe your child here, not with positivity but with … "That must have felt awful and unfair; I am so sorry that happened to you," and then take your child to their body response.

"They said you were weird; that must have felt horrible … When someone says something awful to me, my face starts feeling hot. I get a spinning feeling in my head, and I need to sit down (we do like people using personal stories to convey empathy! Remember … it's often what we do) … Do you remember how that felt when they were so horrible?"

Please keep in mind that many neurodivergents do not experience emotions in the way neurotypicals do … for example, I don't cry when I am sad; I cry when I am overwhelmed. I go mute when I am sad. And sad is such a limited word … How can it be sad that we don't have apples and sad that your best friend is leaving the country forever? That is why using somatic body responses is far more useful than labelling words with generic terms.

When they tell you (sometimes they can't, but that's okay, you've planted a thought seed) … "Okay, so you felt hot and sick. I should have noticed when you walked in you had your hoodie up and looked tense … What did you need me to do?" (99.8087364% of the time, the answer is to stop speaking.)

It's okay if they don't answer … again it gets the brain thinking, 'What do I need? What do I need?' One day, you'll either get an answer, or you'll see a change of behaviour; we don't need to know why.

Wait a few moments. If they don't say anything, wrap it up with a reassuring "I'm sure we'll find the answer together." Offer a connection gesture to show this was not a punitive conversation … something like, "I was about to have some toast, would you like some?" or "I'm going to the shops. Shall I bring you anything, or do you want to come?" anything to show that you are not angry and that your opinion or love for your child has not altered in any way. This may be hard to hear and confusing, but we are convinced with each meltdown that it is THAT meltdown that will be the final straw for you, the one that will make you realise how broken and awful we are. This is why the connection gesture is so powerful and crucial to the process.

Helpful bits at the end of a book 2

Crisis is not always loud. Sometimes it's fawning, shutdown or withdrawal.

Your child has just had a meltdown, and emotions and anxiety are running high … What do you do now?

This is one segment I want everyone to read… a guide to help you during and after the meltdown to keep everybody as emotionally and physically safe as possible.

- The best approach to de-escalating when dealing with an angry child is to **listen** … to try to understand the source of their anger. This allows the child to "flood" and release the angry energy and provides an opportunity to assess and plan an appropriate response.

- **Acknowledge** the child's feelings while not legitimising any harmful behaviour. This approach can diffuse anger quickly.

- It is important to **validate** the child's emotions and **acknowledge** the truth in what is being said when dealing with difficult behaviour.

- **Apologise** sincerely for any mistakes made, but do not try to come up with solutions.

- **Clarify** what the child is saying and repeat their words back to them. This will give them a chance to reflect and possibly explain what they mean.

- The most important thing is to keep the lines of communication open and to understand how deep into a meltdown the child is.

Now let's go through these in more detail.

The first and most important thing is you need to **listen** … Allowing the child to talk and express their feeling – as long as they don't pose a safety risk – is a way of purging the angry energy and helps them to return to a state of equilibrium. I won't pretend that this will be easy; in fact, it can be especially difficult if the language used is offensive or directed at you … But you have to remember; this is not the time to address the language or the behaviour.

Pay attention to what is being said, as it may give you clues as to what triggered the meltdown and what you can do to help de-escalate the situation. Importantly, don't just listen and nod … you will need to respond … **Acknowledge** … They are waiting for you to respond to validate their emotions. Relaying that you understand how they are feeling helps them do just that.

Consider **agreeing** … maybe by saying something like, "Wow, I can see how something like that could cause some anger," or even "If it happened to me, I might be angry too" … This way, you will be confirming the legitimacy of the emotions they are feeling, but not the way they are behaving. Fundamentally, you want them to realise that being angry isn't the problem … the problem is how they choose to act out those angry feelings.

Often when children are angry about something, there is some truth in what they are saying … Try to verify the truth in what is being said and agree with it. This may help them drop their guard, and you consequently eliminate the fuel for the fire. This will again validate their emotions which will, in turn, help diffuse the anger. It is important not to confuse "agreeing" with what is being said with validating inappropriate behaviour … You are simply giving the child the right to be angry, not agreeing that their behaviour is acceptable.

Another important thing to be aware of is never to apologise for an imaginary wrong … However, anything you can spot as being unjust in the situation and **apologising** for it can build credibility as you try to de-escalate. You can, for example, say, "I'm sorry the adults didn't communicate the new plan," … or it can be a simple "I'm sorry you're having such an awful day"… It will go a long way with your child who is having a meltdown and looking for an out. They will know that you're empathetic and may even stop directing their anger towards you as they can see you're trying to help.

Clarify. You should also seek clarity about what is being said. A highly agitated individual may not articulate themselves in a way that was intended or may even have difficulty expressing themselves. Don't make assumptions; instead, try to give the child a chance to clarify what they mean … If they say, "You need to get him out of here before I snap," you can maybe respond with, "Are you saying you're going to hurt him?" The child may then confirm that's what they mean or perhaps deny it, saying, "No. I just don't want to get mad and say something that could get me in trouble." There is a possibility that after listening to their words reflected back, they will want to re-think what they said.

Asking the child to play back the **sequence** of events will encourage them to engage other parts of the brain and be drawn into correcting your version of the events … It may engage the tiger problem-solving part of the brain and can feel empowering too.

Remember that your child is looking for an out; they do not want to feel this way. Giving them an out does not undermine your authority; it helps them feel safe and regulated and, over time, lessens the need for de-escalation.

It is important at this stage to emphasise that if your child could self-regulate independently, they would. They are not disrespecting authority; they genuinely do not understand the concept – being alive longer is not a logical or rational argument.

There are no winners and losers. They are not 'getting' away with anything.

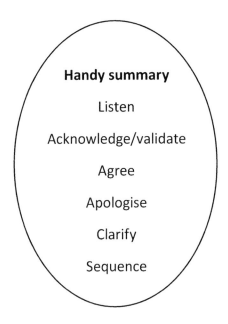

Handy summary

Listen

Acknowledge/validate

Agree

Apologise

Clarify

Sequence

Helpful bits at the end of a book 3

Why rewards and punishments don't work (and, in fact, make things worse)

If you have a rewards and punishment system, you are not alone … but like many other parents, I'm pretty sure you found that they don't work … not for long, anyway. In fact, for the wild children, they seem to make things worse, not to mention appearing to be totally soul-destroying for both you and your children.

Let's start with what you really need to know:

Doing our best is an **adaptive trait**. In the same way that we have adapted to eat to survive, we have adapted to **doing our best** to thrive and succeed.

We are driven by our genes to satisfy five basic needs: **survival**, **love (and belonging), power, freedom, and fun**.

So why doesn't punishment work?

- It encourages children to lie and focus on avoiding punishment rather than working to avoid the behaviour you are trying to stop.

- You tend to need to keep increasing the punishments to make them work. Parents often have a list of punishments they will try to use to control their child's behaviour. Usually, what worked for a while will stop working, prompting you to keep increasing the threats. How far will/can you go?

- Punishment removes the opportunity for your child to reflect and take responsibility for their own behaviour. They tend to see their behaviour as being driven by someone else. They will tend to blame others for what they did and see that they need a parent to control the behaviour.

- You are not addressing what was behind the behaviour in the first place. It doesn't help your child learn to express their emotions; it squashes their needs and sends the message that their feelings aren't important.

- It will damage your relationship with your child. When children feel disconnected from their parents, their motivation to please their parents is gone.

- Punishing a child makes them focus on what is happening to them rather than reflect on why and what they did. They can appear to become more self-centred for survival, hindering the development of empathy for others.

- Your child will feel bad about themselves, not what they did. If your child sees themselves as a "bad" person, it makes sense that they will do "bad" things.

Similarly, rewards won't always work either ... here's why:

- Rewards weaken the ability to self-validate. Your child will rely on you rewarding them to validate their behaviour.

- It feeds insecurity in between rewards.

- Rewards erode the inherent value of everything – learning, doing the right thing, kindness, belonging. Everything.

- It will also hinder creative thinking and problem-solving.

- You will soon notice an increase in the fear of failure.

- Your child will quickly start focusing on outcomes, not learning.

If you look at the research on what we know about human psychology, sticks do not work. Prisons, for example, have a ridiculously high number of re-offenders; it's why it doesn't change behaviour. When we still have a society that is more intent on actual punishment than prevention, and **intrinsic motivation** to learn and succeed, we can see that it simply doesn't work. At best, it's unkind. At worst, it's really, really damaging.

Humans are programmed to do our best regardless; we have learnt that doing our best is the best way to thrive and succeed. The idea that anyone who can self-sabotage on purpose will change their behaviour if we give them a sticker is a complete myth. Remember that children do things for three reasons: they **want** to, they are too **afraid** not to, or they really, really, really **want to please** the caregiver. This third reason can only last so long, and it's the fundamental reason behind masking. Eventually, that mask falls off (or it turns into 'too scared not to.' Do we really want fear to be the driver of our children's actions?).

Think back to the simple example of when a baby says its first word … everyone around them will be excited and may start kissing and hugging the baby. Many children will like the response, and although they didn't do it for the reward, they will think, 'Oh well, I quite like the reaction … I'll do it again.' In the same scenario, a neurodivergent baby will have their motivation confused and may think, 'Hey, I didn't do it for you; I did it for me … I'm not doing THAT again for a week/month/year …'

It's the most paralysing thing on Earth when a neurodivergent person starts getting confused as to why they are doing something. We want to believe we are doing the thing merely because we are driven to, or we simply can't do it again.

Think about a hypervigilant child who is already beginning to mistrust their internal compass because they seem to find themselves getting things wrong ALL THE TIME. Then you give them a reward - let's say a sticker - every time they do something 'right' … For everything they do, when they don't get that sticker, they will feel like they are doing something wrong. Every time someone else gets a sticker … it becomes a judgement on them, and it means they haven't done the right thing. It simply becomes a punishment if other people are getting the reward, and receiving one becomes their only gauge that they are doing something right. There is insecurity between rewards that we didn't realise we introduced. The child (and future adult) ends up living from external validation to external validation, only ever feeling as worthy as their latest sticker.

If all we are trying to do is gain the reward of the very narrow criteria that will get us a sticker … we are not really thinking outside the box. We are actually trying to guess what is in the head of the person who is handing out that reward ... it blocks our thinking about the bigger picture. We are not rewarding the knowledge here ... instead, we are rewarding conformity. We are rewarding knowing what you should say or do rather than rewarding who you are and what you are thinking.

Let's look together at the alternatives, starting with the most important one:

- **Trust your child.** It will take time to reignite their intrinsic motivation.

If the message your child receives is that you trust them to have the answer and do something **but** that you are there if they need help ... this will wake up the part of the brain that will keep trying to find a solution to the problem. They will know that they have the time and the space to work on it.

- **Create a sense of belonging** and **unconditional positive regard.**

Regardless of what's happening, they will know it's okay to struggle or not know... it's okay and actually, their duty to be themselves.

- **Encourage natural outcomes** based on the five basic needs.

There's a big difference between telling a child if they don't behave in a certain way they will not fit in and telling them to think of ways to try and be a part of a group, offering advice but leaving it up to them. You are just giving them information and actions that they can take.

Remember, whatever happens, you are there to support and cradle them … remember that they are trying their best. If your child loses your trust, they will have nothing also to lose … They will never try to adapt their behaviour; they will live within the lines drawn up by a world not made to recognise and celebrate their wonder.

A final note

So, you have made it through my streams of consciousness … what I would love for you is to read them, then reread them … then read them again and again and again … until you don't need them anymore. Until you truly believe and 'know' the sentiment behind them. Until you are no longer afraid …

Once you have internalised their messages, you will never need a strategy again. You will trust your instinct, trust yourself, and most of all, trust that it can really all be okay.

Yes, even on this unconventional path we are walking, even with the storms and avalanches you will battle through along the way … it really will be okay as long as you remember; You have one job … the most natural job in the world … to love them in all their chaos and wonder.

The End

Printed in Great Britain
by Amazon

45918205R00066